ISO

Step b...

A Practical Guide

NAEEM SADIQ
ASIF HAYAT KHAN

IT Governance Publishing

Every possible effort has been made to ensure that the information contained in this book is accurate at the time of going to press, and the publishers and the author cannot accept responsibility for any errors or omissions, however caused. No responsibility for loss or damage occasioned to any person acting, or refraining from action, as a result of the material in this publication can be accepted by the publisher or the author.

Apart from any fair dealing for the purposes of research or private study, or criticism or review, as permitted under the Copyright, Designs and Patents Act 1988, this publication may only be reproduced, stored or transmitted, in any form, or by any means, with the prior permission in writing of the publisher or, in the case of reprographic reproduction, in accordance with the terms of licences issued by the Copyright Licensing Agency. Enquiries concerning reproduction outside those terms should be sent to the publishers at the following address:

IT Governance Publishing
IT Governance Limited
Unit 3, Clive Court
Bartholomew's Walk
Cambridgeshire Business Park
Ely
Cambridgeshire
CB7 4EH
United Kingdom

www.itgovernance.co.uk

The authors have asserted the rights of the author under the Copyright, Designs and Patents Act, 1988, to be identified as the authors of this work.

First published in the United Kingdom in 2011
by IT Governance Publishing.

ISBN 978-1-84928-102-7

FOREWORD

Individuals, organisations and communities across the globe have become increasingly concerned with issues of quality and sustainability of our environment. There is also a growing demand on organisations to demonstrate environmentally responsible behaviour through eco-friendly products, processes and practices.

This book is for all those who wish to develop and implement an effective ISO14001-based environment management system (EMS). International standards, such as ISO14001, often carry a formality about them with each word bearing a specific meaning and context. They define requirements on 'what' ought to be done, without prescribing any specific details on 'how' it might be achieved. There is, therefore, a need to demystify the ISO14001 standard by presenting its requirements, as well as its implementation methodology, in a simple, user-friendly and easily understandable manner.

This guide is ideal for managers, auditors and trainers who are involved in any aspect of an ISO14001-based management system – may it be development, implementation, training or auditing. The guide takes a hands-on and step-by-step approach. It explains the purpose and the requirement of each clause and describes how the requirements may be fulfilled by an organisation. It includes numerous examples, suggestions and samples of documentation to facilitate understanding and implementation for those who may not have a strong background to this subject.

ABOUT THE AUTHORS

Naeem Sadiq holds a BSc in Aerospace and a Masters in Manufacturing Engineering. Mr Sadiq is a certified lead auditor and lead trainer for ISO9001, ISO14001 and OHSAS18001 standards. He is also an ASQ certified manager and quality system auditor.

Naeem's work experience in engineering and management includes working as an independent consultant, auditor and trainer for ISO9001, ISO14001 and OHSAS18001 standards.

He has presented a number of papers in national conferences on management system standards, and provided consultancy, training and auditing support to over 100 organisations. As a freelance writer, he is a regular contributor to a national newspaper on environmental and social issues.

Asif Hayat Khan holds a BSc in Industrial Engineering. Mr Khan is a trained lead auditor and trainer for ISO9001, ISO14001 and OHSAS18001 standards. He is also an ASQ certified quality manager, HACCP auditor and a DuPont certified trainer on behavioural safety.

As a consultant, auditor, trainer and manager, he has experience of establishing and implementing ISO9001, ISO14001 and OHSAS18001 standards in diverse industrial sectors.

ACKNOWLEDGEMENTS

We deeply acknowledge all those organisations and people with whom we have had the privilege of working, training, consulting and auditing. These rich and varied experiences helped us in our own learning and understanding, without which this book would not have been possible.

x

DISCLAIMER

All names, examples and values quoted in this book are fictitious and have been presented for learning, understanding and explaining purposes only.

Websites quoted in this book may change over a period of time and users may need to look up new addresses where a change has taken place.

CONTENTS

Chapter 1: Environmental Policy, Objectives and Programmes (Clauses 4.2 & 4.3.3).....................1

Chapter 2: Identifying Environmental Aspects and Determining Significant Impacts (Clause 4.3.1)9

Chapter 3: Regulatory Requirements and Evaluation of Compliance (Clauses 4.3.2 & 4.5.2).................13

Chapter 4: Resources, Roles, Responsibility, Authority and Communication (Clause 4.4.1 & 4.4.3)............17

Chapter 5: Competence, Training and Awareness (Clause 4.4.2)...21

Chapter 6: Documentation, Document Control and Records (Clause 4.3.1)......................................25

Chapter 7: Operational Controls (Clause 4.4.6)29

Chapter 8: Emergency Preparedness and Response (Clause 4.4.7)..33

Chapter 9: Measuring and Monitoring (Clause 4.5.1) 37

Chapter 10: Non-conformity, Corrective and Preventative Action (Clause 4.5.3)..39

Chapter 11: Internal Audit (Clause 4.5.5)......43

Chapter 12: Management Review and Continual Improvement (Clause 4.5.6)............................47

Chapter 13: Green Initiatives..........................51

Appendix A: Sample Procedure for Identification of Environmental Aspects......................................57

Appendix B: Sample Procedure for Internal and External Communication...63

Appendix C: Sample Procedure for Control of Documents and Records...65

Appendix D: Documents Required by ISO14001   69

Appendix E: Records Required by ISO14001 73

Appendix F: Sample Format for a Non-conformity Report (NCR)...75

Appendix G: Sample Procedure for Internal EMS Audit...79

Appendix H: Sample Input Report for EMS Management Review...83

Bibliographic Notes 91

ITG Resources..93

Environmental policy

An environmental policy is a statement of an organisation's top management commitment, which defines the direction and intentions of the organisation with regard to its environmental performance. The policy must be consistent with the nature, scale and environmental impacts of the organisation's activities, products and services – and must be approved by the top management.

Summary of requirements

The following diagram provides an overview of what an environmental management system (EMS) policy statement must contain:

Figure 1: EMS policy requirements

How can this requirement be met by an organisation?

The following points define what an organisation is required to do in order to meet the requirements of the standard:

- Top management must document and approve an environmental policy that reflects its vision and commitment to being an environmentally responsible company.
- The EMS policy must be communicated to all employees. An organisation can choose many methods to communicate its policy, such as training sessions, video messages, displays at prominent locations, newsletters, embedded in e-mails, etc.
- Top management must review the EMS policy at planned intervals to ensure its continued suitability and adequacy.

An example of an environmental policy is shown below:

Eco-Friendly Inc. (EFI) environmental policy

EFI is committed to providing fast-moving home use products in an environmentally responsible manner. The company will fulfil its environmental commitment by:

- assessing the environmental risks and operating the business in a way that ensures prevention of pollution through the application of economically viable best available environmental practices
- ensuring compliance with applicable environmental legislation
- collaborating with suppliers for sustainable sourcing of raw materials, as well as with the transporters, carriers, business partners and other concerned organisations for improving end-to-end environmental performance
- continually improving products, processes and ways of doing business which reduce levels of environmental impact through sustainable initiatives, such as energy, water and natural

resources conservation, waste and gaseous emissions reduction (particularly the greenhouse gases), and exploring opportunities for reuse and recycling.

Objective, targets and programmes

Summary of requirements

- The organisation is required to set goals that it wants to achieve with regard to its environmental performance and set targets to meet those goals.
- The organisation shall also establish and implement programs for achieving its objectives and targets.

Considerations while setting environmental objectives and targets

While setting objectives and targets, the organisation must consider the following:

- **EMS policy:** top management's commitment and vision, as stated in the company's EMS policy.
- **Significant environmental aspects:** targets and objectives must be set for the aspects where existing control measures are not sufficient and where environmental risk is either not tolerable, or not likely to remain tolerable in the near future.
- **Legal and other requirements:** if an organisation is currently not meeting, or not likely to meet, any of the legal requirements pertaining to its environmental management system, it should consider establishing objectives to improve its performance relating to these requirements.
- **Technological options and financial considerations:** needless to say, the organisation should consider technological options and financial viability while establishing EMS improvement objectives.
- **Operational and business requirements and views of interested parties:** these are yet other factors for

consideration while establishing EMS objectives. Environmental concerns, such as coastal and marine life, banning chromium from the leather industry, using environmentally friendly dyes in textiles and garments, and minimising the use of non-biodegradable plastic, noise, smoke or traffic congestion often raised by interested parties, ought to be considered while establishing EMS objectives.

Some examples of EMS objectives and targets are shown in *Figure 2*, overleaf.

Objectives	Targets
Removal of ozone depleting substances from operations	100% removal by 2015
Reduction in water consumed per ton of production	Reduce from current consumption level of 5 m^3/ton to 4 m^3/ton of production by December 2011
Effluent treatment plant expansion to cater for enhanced production volume projected for 2013	Existing capacity = 10 tonnes per hour Target = 15 tonnes per hour by December 2013

Figure 2: EMS objectives and targets

Environmental programmes

An environmental programme is a roadmap or a plan for achieving an environmental objective. It defines responsibilities, means and time-frames by which the objectives are to be achieved. An example of an environmental programme is given in *Figure 3*, overleaf.

Objective: reduce water consumption from the current baseline of 15,000 gallons per month per 100 tonnes of production, to 12,000 gallons per month per 100 tonnes of production by July 2011			
No.	**Actions/projects**	**Responsibility**	**Target date**
1	Replace hosepipe floor cleaning with vacuum cleaner	Admin Manager	March 2010
2	Recycle treated and grey water for factory plantation	Engineering Manager	Dec. 2010
3	Install auto-taps in the washrooms	Engineering Manager	Jan. 2011
4	Replace shower system for cleaning of product with dip cleaning	Engineering Manager	June 2011

Figure 3: Example environmental programme

Measurement, monitoring and changes to environmental objectives, targets and programmes

The organisation is required to monitor the extent to which its environmental objectives and targets have been met. This information must be fed to the top management for review of the EMS. This information may be needed to ascertain:

- whether the objectives and targets are being achieved as planned
- whether there is a need for additional resources
- whether there is a need to modify the planned objectives, targets and programmes.

CHAPTER 2: IDENTIFYING ENVIRONMENTAL ASPECTS AND DETERMINING SIGNIFICANT IMPACTS (CLAUSE 4.3.1)

Summary of requirements

Establish and implement procedure(s) to:

- identify environmental aspects of all activities, products and services that are performed within the defined scope of the organisation
- determine those that have or can have significant impacts on the environment
- establish an EMS which must be based on consideration of the significant environmental aspects.

Terms used

Environment: because of its products, processes and activities, an organisation constantly interacts with its surroundings. These interactions could relate to water, air, land, natural resources or even flora, fauna, aquatic life or community. The complete set of surroundings in which an organisation operates may be considered its environment.

Environmental aspect: an organisation may interact with environments in many ways. These could relate to the activities that it carries out, the products that it makes and the processes that it uses to make these products. Any such component that interacts with the environment is considered to be an environmental aspect of the organisation.

There are two types of environmental aspects:

- **direct environmental aspects:** those aspects over which a company can be expected to have an influence and control, for example, emissions from its processes
- **indirect environmental aspects:** those aspects over which the organisation can be expected to have an influence, but no control, for example, energy

consumption for the production of raw materials or emissions from trucks used by suppliers.

How can these requirements be met by an organisation?

- Begin by establishing a cross-functional environmental aspect and impact assessment team. Team members must be familiar with environmental issues, laws, the processes under study and the procedure for determining aspects and impacts.
- Document a procedure that defines the complete process for identification of aspects and impacts. A sample procedure is shown in *Appendix A*.
- Make an inventory of all processes, products and activities (routine, non-routine, normal, abnormal and emergency) performed by an organisation.
- Identify inputs and outputs of each process, product and activity.
- Identify environmental aspects of each input and output using a black box approach, as shown in *Figure 4*.

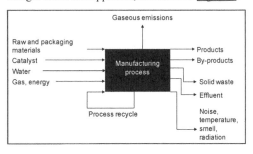

**Figure 4: Identification of environmental aspects –
the input-output approach**

- The environmental aspects could be:
  - emissions to air
  - release to water
  - waste management and disposal

- o   contamination of land
- o   impact on communities
- o   use of raw materials, energy and natural resources
- o   use of ozone depletion or radioactive materials
- o   other local environmental and community issues.

- Determine the environmental impact of each aspect. While determining environmental impacts, give due consideration to controls already in place, severity, frequency, legal requirements, and impact on company image. A sample environmental significance rating system is described in *Appendix A*.
- Document aspects and impacts in a register of significant environmental aspects (*see Table 2 of Appendix A for sample format*).
- Review the register of significant environmental aspects as an ongoing activity (say once every year). Also review the register when new aspects are identified, when an environmental incident takes place, or whenever processes and activities are added or modified.
- Consider significant environmental aspects while establishing the EMS of the company. The significant environmental aspects should form the basis of the EMS objective-setting process. The significant environmental aspects must also be considered while establishing other elements of the environmental system, such as training, operational controls, measuring and monitoring, structure and responsibility, emergency preparedness, audits and management reviews.
- Consider environmental aspects and their significance while designing new products and processes. Such assessments should also be conducted prior to making any changes in existing processes and activities.

CHAPTER 3: REGULATORY REQUIREMENTS AND EVALUATION OF COMPLIANCE (CLAUSES 4.3.2 & 4.5.2)

Summary of requirements

Establish and implement a system that:

- defines the process of identification and access to applicable legal and other requirements to which the organisation subscribes (relating to its environmental aspects)
- determines the extent of applicability of these requirements
- considers these requirements while establishing and implementing the environmental system
- periodically verifies the organisation's continued compliance to these requirements.

How can these requirements be met by an organisation?

The first step in managing compliance with environmental legal requirements is to know which requirements are applicable to the environmental aspects of an organisation's activities, products and services.

Each country has its own environmental laws and regulatory bodies. The three environmental regulators in the UK are: the Environment Agency for England and Wales (EA), the Scottish Environment Protection Agency (SEPA) and the Environment and Heritage Service Northern Ireland (EHS NI). A good source of regulatory information is NetRegs (_www.netregs.gov.uk_), a web-based tool developed by these three organisations.

Laws relating to local authorities, such as land use planning, local air quality strategies (to reflect the national air quality strategy), Local Authority Air Pollution Control (LAAPC), clean air acts, noise and statutory nuisance and tree preservation orders should also be reviewed for possible applicability.

Environmental regulations are often implemented by the regulators by issuing environmental permits that contain conditions that the permit holder must fulfil. These are normally applied to operations at specific sites or installations, and typically regulate emissions to air (e.g. local authority air pollution control), water (e.g. consents to discharge) and land (e.g. waste management licences). Pollution Prevention and Control (PPC) permits are used to regulate all media on an integrated basis.

It is the responsibility of an organisation to apply for an environmental permit that is applicable and required under the law.

This clause of the standard requires an organisation to define and implement a procedure that describes how an organisation identifies and implements the following activities:

- Identify all environmental laws, conventions, permits and licences that are applicable to its products, processes, outputs, liquid discharges, solid waste, emissions and activities. Not every regulatory requirement is applicable to all organisations. An organisation, therefore, needs to determine those requirements that are applicable to its own products, processes and activities. A list of such applicable laws and requirements should be made and kept updated.
- Identify how an organisation accesses the sources (departments, ministries, websites, groups, organisations) that create or issue this information. The purpose of this requirement is to ensure that an organisation can access all sources on an ongoing basis to keep itself abreast of the latest regulatory and other applicable requirements.
- Regulatory requirements play an important role in defining an EMS. Being mandatory in nature, the legal requirements add to the significance of environmental aspects. Therefore, it is necessary that an organisation considers legal requirements while establishing its

environmental objectives and programmes. Training, measuring, monitoring, communication, organisational structure, operational controls and responsibilities are the other elements that will normally be influenced by applicable environmental laws.

- ISO14001 requires that an organisation must periodically evaluate (periodicity may be defined by law or by the organisation) its compliance against all applicable environmental laws and other requirements to which it subscribes. The mechanism and responsibility for performing this task must be defined by the organisation.

Some of the websites that could provide useful regulatory information about applicable environmental laws in the UK, Germany, USA, Canada, Australia and China are given below:

United Kingdom

NetRegs

- *www.netregs.gov.uk*

The Environment Agency

- *www.environment-agency.gov.uk/business/topics/permitting/118404.aspx*
- *www.environment-agency.gov.uk/business/topics/permitting/32334.aspx*
- *www.environment-agency.gov.uk/business/regulation/38807.aspx*

Environmental Protection UK

- *www.environmental-protection.org.uk/air-quality-and-climate/air-quality/laws/*

Department for Environment Food and Rural Affairs (DEFRA)

- *www.defra.gov.uk/environment/waste/*

Germany

- *www.umweltbundesamt.de/umweltrecht-e/verbandsklage/index.htm*

USA

- *www.epa.gov/lawsregs/*

Canada

- *www.ec.gc.ca/default.asp?lang=En&n=48D356C1-1*

Australia

- *www.environment.gov.au/about/legislation.html*

China

- *http://english.mep.gov.cn/Policies_Regulations/*

Records to be kept

The following records must be maintained by an organisation:

- an updated list of all applicable environmental regulatory and other requirements to which an organisation subscribes
- results of measuring, monitoring and testing, carried out at defined frequency to demonstrate that the organisation complies with all environmental regulatory and other applicable requirements.

CHAPTER 4: RESOURCES, ROLES, RESPONSIBILITY, AUTHORITY AND COMMUNICATION (CLAUSE 4.4.1 & 4.4.3)

Summary of requirements

- Provide resources required to establish, implement, maintain and improve the EMS.
- Define roles and responsibilities and appoint specific management representative(s) for EMS.
- Establish procedure(s) that define processes for internal as well as external communication.

How can these requirements be met by an organisation?

An EMS system can neither be implemented nor improved, unless the required human, financial, material, specialised skills and organisational resources are provided by the management. This may be done in the following manner:

- The senior management defines the organisation's structure, and the roles, responsibilities and authorities of all those who are required to perform any task relating to EMS. These could be tasks relating to identifying significant environmental aspects, establishing EMS objectives, ensuring the application of EMS controls, planning, measuring and monitoring EMS performance, training, communicating with internal and external bodies, ensuring compliance, etc.
- The next step is to ensure that the individuals are competent to perform their assigned roles. (*See Chapter 5 for competency requirements.*)
- Top management must nominate a competent person as a 'management representative'. He must have the authority to ensure that EMS is established, implemented and maintained according to the requirements of ISO14001. He must also report the performance of the EMS to top management for review and further improvement. (*See Chapter 12 on elements that constitute this report.*) Some

aspects of a management representative's competence could include knowledge of environmental issues, the ISO14001 standard, environmental controls and good communication skills.

Communication

In order to implement an effective EMS, an organisation must communicate internally as well as externally.

Internal communication

The internal communication focuses on communication within the company and could entail:

- awareness and training on all EMS issues, requirements and procedures at various levels within the organisation
- communication of regulatory requirements to all concerned
- receiving feedback on measurement and monitoring of EMS performance
- communication of the results of EMS performance to top management
- ensuring that people at all levels and in all functions receive the needed EMS information in a reasonable time-frame.
- ensuring that employees are able to forward suggestions and EMS concerns to the concerned management.

The following list provides numerous examples of internal communication:

- displays on bulletin boards of the key EMS goals and the extent to which they have been achieved
- regular EMS meetings, at various levels of management and for various levels of employees to discuss and review EMS issues
- training sessions
- reporting EMS performance to top management

- e-mail messages and notes in salary slips that inform employees about EMS initiatives
- suggestion boxes
- newsletters.

External communication

A company may also have many external stakeholders that it communicates with. These could be customers, vendors, suppliers, contractors, neighbours, environmental groups and regulators.

External communication could entail:

- receiving and responding to concerns of interested parties, such as NGOs, environmental groups and communities
- communicating with regulatory and environmental protection agencies
- communications relating to permits, licences and fines.

A sample procedure on communication is placed in *Appendix B*.

The organisation has the choice to decide whether it wishes to communicate externally about its significant environmental aspects. If it does decide to do so, it must define who and how this communication will take place.

Examples of external communication:

- maintaining a website that describes company EMS policy and initiatives
- meetings with vendors and suppliers to explore options for environmentally friendly products
- informing customers about EMS initiatives of the company and influencing them to do the same
- participating in community meetings
- receiving and responding to government and regulatory agencies.

CHAPTER 5: COMPETENCE, TRAINING AND AWARENESS (CLAUSE 4.4.2)

Summary of requirements

- People performing tasks that relate to potentially significant environmental impacts must be competent to perform those tasks.
- Identify and provide training associated with EMS as well as environmental aspects.
- Establish procedure(s) to provide awareness relating to significant aspects, EMS policy, objectives and procedures, including the potential consequences of not complying with these procedures.

How can these requirements be met by an organisation?

This clause aims to provide for competence of all personnel who perform tasks, for or on behalf of the organisation, that have the potential to cause a significant environmental impact. The following step-by-step approach, backed up by a procedure could effectively meet the requirements of this clause:

- Identify all those individuals who perform tasks that have a potential to cause significant environmental impacts. *Figure 5* explains how inputs from many elements of EMS contribute to the training needs analysis process.

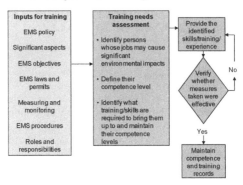

Figure 5: Training needs assessment

- The main thrust of this clause is to ensure that all personnel are aware of their environmental roles and responsibilities, they have adequate competence to perform them effectively and they understand the potential consequences of departure from specified procedures. This should include employees as well as those who perform work for the company, such as contractors.

- Make a list of all EMS tasks that ought to be undertaken at all levels in the company that have the potential to cause significant environmental impact. The environmental tasks considered should include those performed routinely, as well as those performed in emergency situations.

- It is important to verify whether the training/skills provided, or other actions taken, did in fact result in achieving the intended goal. There are many methods that may be used to determine the effectiveness of actions taken. These could range from a simple examination for theoretical subjects to practical testing for skill-based subjects.

- Keep records of training provided. These could be records relating to training needs analyses, training calendars, attendance sheets, certificates or records of training effectiveness.

CHAPTER 6: DOCUMENTATION, DOCUMENT CONTROL AND RECORDS (CLAUSE 4.3.1)

It is necessary to understand the difference between the terms 'document' and 'record' before proceeding to the main contents of this chapter.

Documents provide information, data or instructions and could be on any medium, such as print or electronic. Some examples of documents are:

- policies, objectives, targets, programmes or plans
- manuals and procedures
- work instructions or standard operating procedures
- photographs, videos or drawings providing instructions
- legal requirements
- formats and checklists (when blank).

Records are a special category of documents. They provide evidence, results or facts relating to actions that have been taken by an organisation. Some examples of records are:

- training records
- driver's licence
- machine maintenance records
- results of effluent, emission or solid waste discharge tests
- audit results, non-conformity reports
- minutes of management review meetings
- photographs, videos or drawings providing evidence (flight data recorder, CCTV images, etc.).

Summary of requirements

- The organisation shall establish documents and records required by ISO14001, as well as those that relate to its own significant environmental aspects.
- In addition, the following documents shall also be established:
    - EMS scope, policy, objectives and targets

- o description of the main elements of the EMS and their interaction
- o reference to related documents
- o procedure(s) for control of organisational documents, documents of external origin, as well as maintenance and retention of records.

How can these requirements be met by an organisation?

EMS scope

Organisations need to define the scope of their EMS in order to establish the boundaries of all that is included in the system. Typically, the EMS scope will include all of the organisation's activities that take place on its premises; those areas that are under its direct control, and those where it has environmental regulatory liability. The scope may also include areas that are outside the organisation's direct control, but over which it may be able to exert some influence, such as encouraging employees to use carpooling or mass transportation systems when travelling to and from work.

An example of a company's EMS scope could be:

Eco-Friendly Inc, located at 300 Minnesota Avenue, Kansas City, Kansas is engaged in the manufacture and sale of fast-moving home use products.

Description of the main elements of EMS and their interactions

The documentation should define the main elements of the EMS and their interaction, and include or provide reference to related documents. Interaction of elements may be described in any suitable manner, such as describing them in words, making flow charts or block diagrams. The core document that includes the scope of EMS and the description and interactions of its elements is often referred to as the EMS manual.

EMS documents

The standard refers to two types of documents and records needed for an EMS: those that are mentioned within the standard as mandatory requirements and those that are needed by an individual organisation for effective management of its EMS. The procedure for internal EMS audit is an example of a mandatory document (required by ISO14001), while a procedure for cleaning a scrubber is an example of a document needed by an organisation for effective management of its EMS.

Control of documents and records

An organisation needs to establish documented procedure(s) for controlling its documents (Clause 4.4.5) and records (Clause 4.5.4). Organisations may either choose to define separate procedures for control of documents and records, or an integrated procedure that includes both.

The issues addressed by a document and record control procedure are described in a sample procedure placed at *Appendix C*.

Appendix D describes the documents required by ISO14001, while *Appendix E* describes the records required by the ISO14001 standard.

CHAPTER 7: OPERATIONAL CONTROLS (CLAUSE 4.4.6)

What are operational controls?

Operational controls may be defined as 'measures taken to manage risks'. In the context of environmental management systems, 'operational controls' will be referred to as the methods and means implemented for managing environmental risks, where their absence could lead to:

- deviation from the company's environmental policy, objectives and targets
- violation of specified legal or other applicable requirements
- environmental pollution.

The following diagram explains the requirement of operational controls:

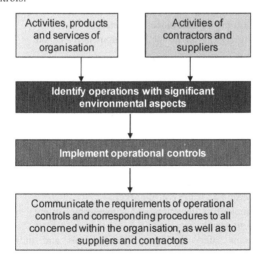

Figure 6: Operational controls

Types of operational controls

Operational controls may be broadly categorised as administrative controls or engineering controls.

Administrative controls include:

- written procedures or instructions (operations, waste/effluent/emission/hazardous substance management, utilities, etc.)
- supervision
- competence or training requirements
- permit to work (PTW)
- own or contractor's environmental control procedures (induction training, meetings, inspections, access control, PTW systems, etc.)
- inspection and maintenance programmes
- solid waste disposal procedures
- fire watch
- emergency preparedness procedures and drills
- spill control and treatment procedures (equipment, neutralising substances, kits, etc.)
- use of personal protective equipment (PPE), etc.

Engineering controls include:

- isolation and enclosure of environmentally hazardous materials
- containment walls for hazardous liquids (chemicals, flammables)
- leak detection and alarm systems
- electronic or mechanical interlocks to prevent emissions, overflows or spills
- line evacuation systems (pigging, etc.) to minimise solid waste and water consumption
- smoke/fire detection and suppression systems such as auto sprinklers
- plant safety devices (visual controls and indicators, non-return valves, pressure relief systems, etc.)
- emergency shutdown systems
- effluent treatment plants

- scrubbers and sprays to reduce particulate matter and other hazardous gases from emissions.

While selecting operational controls the organisation should consider the following hierarchy:

- elimination (e.g. lead free petrol, chrome free leather)
- reduction (recycle, reuse or substitute, e.g. reducing paper thickness in packaging, recycling grey water for plantation, reusing printing toners, substituting incandescent bulbs with LED lights)
- isolation (enclosure/segregation, e.g. building a containment wall around fuel storage, separate containers to collect different types of wastage)
- control (through administrative and/or engineering controls)
- defences (e.g. personal protective equipment, emergency procedures, fire-fighting, spill management).

CHAPTER 8: EMERGENCY PREPAREDNESS AND RESPONSE (CLAUSE 4.4.7)

Summary of requirements

The organisation shall establish and implement procedure(s) that identify potential emergency situations (that could negatively impact upon the environment), and also define mechanisms to respond to these situations. These actions must include mitigation of any adverse environmental impacts.

The organisation must also periodically review and test these procedures.

How can these requirements be met by an organisation?

There are two main components to this clause, namely 'preparedness' and 'response'.

Preparedness

- With a group of individuals from various functional areas in the organisation, it is important to brainstorm possible EMS accidents and emergencies.
- Review incident records for past years. Also review the environmental aspects list for potential emergencies under abnormal operating conditions. Some examples of potential environmental emergencies/accidents are:
  o a hazardous gas leak
  o a fire or explosion
  o unplanned emissions or effluent discharges
  o a spill
  o failure of a tank, dam, equipment or structure
  o a natural disaster – lightning, earthquake, flood, extreme weather
  o a crash or collision
  o sabotage, vandalism, terrorist attack, bomb threat or riot

- o   any other impact arising out of hazardous substances handled, stored or used in the organisation.
- Identify and list all potential emergencies and accidents that could be encountered by an organisation.
- Determine what is required to respond to these emergency situations. This could include establishing and implementing the following:
  - o   an emergency organisation and its roles and responsibilities
  - o   the resources and the equipment needed to respond and take actions to prevent or mitigate the associated environmental impacts. These could include spill kits to contain the spread of harmful liquids, suction pumps, equipment for removal of contaminated soil, etc.
  - o   emergency procedures that must be adopted by all persons
  - o   the training of personnel on emergency procedures and actions
  - o   the information and communication processes needed in an emergency, which may include maps/drawings of electrical cabling, gas pipes, underground tanks, storm water channels, containment pits, etc.
  - o   the liaison and support needed from external agencies, such as the police, fire brigade, hospitals and concerned environmental agencies.
- Potential locations where an emergency can occur should be mapped, and emergency equipment located nearby.
- Neighbourhood areas vulnerable to gas escape or other consequences of an emergency at the facility should also be identified and marked on a map for rapid notification or other relief/mitigation actions. Prevailing wind directions should be mapped to identify the potential downwind areas. Sensitive areas in the vicinity may include residential, industrial, agricultural, recreation, fishing areas or sanctuaries.
- Emergency exits and muster points should be identified and marked.

Response

The standard requires an organisation to implement mechanisms to respond to accidents or emergencies by taking actions to prevent or mitigate associated adverse environmental impacts. However, any effective response would require not just preparedness, but also prior rehearsals and drills of the procedures to make sure that:

- the procedures are adequate and can effectively respond to a real emergency or accident
- all persons understand their roles and know how to perform them in emergency situations
- the emergency equipment gets tested and its condition gets known.

An organisation must test its emergency procedures by simulating various kinds of identified emergencies under as real conditions as practicable. Such drills do not have any learning value unless they are closely monitored for accomplishment of their key performance parameters, e.g. response time, ability to contain a spill, fire-fighting, effectiveness of equipment, ability to evacuate and effectiveness of mitigation measures. Results of such drills must be maintained and analysed for further improvement of the emergency response system.

Emergency procedures must be reviewed at planned intervals and also after the occurrence of an accident or an emergency. This is done to ensure continuing adequacy and suitability of the emergency preparedness and response procedures.

CHAPTER 9: MEASURING AND MONITORING (CLAUSE 4.5.1)

Summary of requirements

It is necessary to establish and implement procedure(s) to measure and monitor those aspects of EMS performance that could have significant environmental impacts.

How can these requirements be met by an organisation?

The measurement and monitoring process must be viewed in a larger context and its scope extended to the entire environmental system. An organisation needs to define mechanisms and responsibilities for ongoing measuring and monitoring of key characteristics of those processes and activities that have the potential for significant environmental impacts.

Key characteristics are those characteristics that provide vital information or can have significant influence on the environmental performance of the process, and thus need to be measured or monitored. These may be the amount of effluent discharged; the amount of biological oxygen demand (BOD) or chemical oxygen demand (COD) in outgoing effluent; the number of spills; temperature limits in a chemical warehouse; the amount of hazardous waste; unplanned releases; the quantity of toxic chemicals released; the amount of fuel, gas, electricity or water used, etc.

They also need to define mechanisms and responsibilities for regular monitoring/measuring of the following:

- the equipment used in emergency situations, spill kits, smoke detectors, fire detection and fire control systems
- controls whose absence or failure could cause significant environmental impacts (e.g. relief valves, one-way valves, pressure and temperature sensors, auto warning

signals, pressure vessel inspections, critical inspections, permits to work, controls over suppliers and contractors)
- the extent to which the environmental objectives and targets have been achieved
- chemical, fuel and hazardous waste handling, storage and disposal methods
- training needs, training conducted, employee awareness and competence
- communications from interested parties
- effectiveness of emergency response measures
- effectiveness of corrective and preventative actions
- environmental performance of contractors.

A measuring and monitoring plan should form the core of the measuring and monitoring process. The plan should include:

- parameters to be measured/monitored
- responsibility for measurement/monitoring
- procedure used for measurement/monitoring
- frequency of measuring/monitoring
- records to be kept.

CHAPTER 10: NON-CONFORMITY, CORRECTIVE AND PREVENTATIVE ACTION (CLAUSE 4.5.3)

Summary of requirements

- The organisation shall establish a system for actions to be taken when a real or a potential non-conformity is determined.
- Investigate and determine the causes of non-conformities, take corrective or preventative actions (as applicable) and determine effectiveness of actions taken. Mitigation of environmental impacts is an integral part of corrective actions.

How can these requirements be met by an organisation?

It is best to explain in straightforward words the meaning of terms used in this chapter.

- **Corrective actions** involve correcting an existing non-conformity, determining its root cause and taking actions to prevent its recurrence.
- **Preventative actions** involve taking actions to eliminate the causes of potential non-conformities to prevent their occurrence.
- **Non-conformity** is non-fulfilment of a requirement stated in law, standards or an organisation's own procedures.

An organisation may identify existing environmental non-conformities from any of the following sources:

- while conducting an internal or external environmental audit
- while measuring, monitoring or testing for compliance or any other requirement
- after an environmental incident occurs (spill, release, etc.)

- after a complaint from a regulatory body or any other interested party.

An organisation may identify potential environmental non-conformities (opportunities for preventative actions) from any of the following sources:

- data collection and analysis of environmental measurement and monitoring
- design stage of new processes and products
- actions arising out of EMS leading indicators (initiatives for environmental system improvement or upkeep).

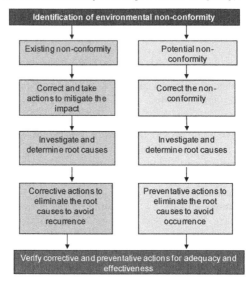

Figure 7: Corrective and preventative action cycle

Once an existing or potential non-conformity has been identified, the following steps must be implemented.

- Take actions to correct the non-conformity as well as mitigate environmental impacts, if any. This may include containment, clean-up activities, compensations, etc.
- Investigate and identify the root causes of the non-conformity. It is necessary to differentiate between immediate, direct and root causes. Consider, as an example, a fuel spill caused by the turning over of a fuel tank lorry. While the turning over of fuel tank lorry is the immediate cause, rash driving could be the direct cause and lack of training, inadequate knowledge of speed limits and absence of route risk assessment could be the root causes. Often there is more than one root cause that contributes to an incident, and all must be explored.
- Take actions to eliminate the root cause(s) so as to prevent recurrence of the non-conformity. This requires addressing the direct causes as well as the root causes.
- Verify actions taken for adequacy and effectiveness. Often problems reoccur if the corrective actions taken are not adequate or effective. The verification process is, therefore, a way of evaluating whether all holes (root causes) have been plugged. Verification for effectiveness of corrective actions should be done by someone competent in root cause analysis tools, such as 'cause and effect diagrams', 'why-why analysis', 'failure mode and effect analysis', statistical tools, etc.
- Records must be maintained of corrective/ preventative actions.

Appendix F describes a suggested format of non-conformity.

CHAPTER 11: INTERNAL AUDIT (CLAUSE 4.5.5)

Summary of requirements

- Establish audit procedure(s) that define the responsibilities for planning, conducting, reporting, follow-up, frequency, scope and process for conducting internal environmental audits.
- The organisation shall ensure that internal EMS audits are conducted at planned intervals.
- The audits shall determine whether the EMS conforms to the planned arrangements and the requirements of ISO14001. Audits must also determine whether the EMS has been implemented effectively.
- Auditors shall be objective and impartial.

How can these requirements be met by the organisation?

It is best to begin by seeking clarity on the meaning of terms used in the audit process:

- **Audits** are intended to determine the extent to which an organisational system complies with its criteria. Audits must be carried out by those who are themselves not directly responsible for the activity under audit. The process of evidence collection and evaluation against the criteria must be carried out in a planned, documented and objective manner.
- **Audit criteria** represent a set of requirements against which the audit is carried out.
- **Audit findings** are what an auditor determines after comparing and evaluating the evidence with the criteria against which the audit was carried out. An audit finding could result in a 'conforming', or a 'non-conforming' situation.

Implementing an internal EMS audit process in a company requires the following steps to be undertaken:

- Begin by establishing an internal EMS audit procedure. A sample audit procedure is placed at *Appendix G*.
- Nominate a competent person to assume overall responsibility for ensuring the tasks involved in audit planning, conducting, reporting and follow-up are implemented effectively.
- Prepare an audit plan, which reflects the frequency and the scope of audit. Give due consideration to the importance of activities and results of previous audits while making the audit plan.
- Select and train a team of auditors who could be used for conducting audits. The competence of auditors plays an important role in quality and output of audits and, therefore, it would be worthwhile investing in auditor training and competence. A good auditor training programme could be spread over three to five days and include topics like EMS issues, the ISO14001 standard, audit principles, audit communication and audit planning, conducting and reporting.
- Share the audit plan with auditors and auditees. Auditors must prepare themselves by gaining awareness about auditee's processes and documentation before the start of the audit. Knowledge of applicable regulatory requirements and preparation of checklists can add great value to the conduct of an EMS audit.
- Audits are best conducted on a process-based approach. This shifts the focus from narrow, procedure-oriented hair splitting to the bigger EMS issues. In simple terms an audit should gather evidence to determine the following:
  - Does the organisation meet the requirements defined in ISO14001?
  - Does the EMS enable an organisation to meet its environmental objectives and planned arrangements (could include company policies, procedures and controls)?
  - Does the EMS enable a company to prevent pollution and comply with legal and other requirements?

- o Is the EMS implemented effectively and continually improved?
- The independence of auditors is mandatory and can be ensured by not nominating an auditor for an activity that falls under his/her own area of responsibility.
- The auditors must be encouraged to adopt a friendly, professional and open approach to the audit process. It is good to keep an auditee aware of how and what findings are being arrived at. An auditee prefers to have a sense of participation in the audit process and also does not wish to receive surprises at the end of the day.
- A critical skill of an auditor is his ability to verify the effectiveness of corrective actions. This must include considerations such as:
  - o Have the root cause(s) been identified correctly?
  - o Will the actions taken ensure that the audit non-conformity will not reoccur?
  - o Have other similar situations, tasks, locations and equipment been also reviewed for removal of the same or similar nonconformity. A non-conformity is like a bad fish in a pond. Removing some and not others will surely spoil the remaining fish in due course.
  - o Have the issues of shortcomings in training, organisational structure, adequacy of resources and management commitment been also considered and addressed.

CHAPTER 12: MANAGEMENT REVIEW AND CONTINUAL IMPROVEMENT (CLAUSE 4.5.6)

Summary of requirements

- It is the responsibility of top management to review the performance of its EMS at defined intervals.
- The review is intended to determine how well the system is performing and how it can be improved further.
- The review must be based on inputs, such as audit results, legal compliance, communication(s) with interested parties, objectives, corrective and preventative actions, and recommendations for improvement.
- The top management should provide specific decisions and actions relating to continual improvements in the EMS.

How can these requirements be met by an organisation?

'Management review' is the final platform upon which the performance and adequacy of the EMS is reviewed. Issues not reviewed in, or missed out of, the management review will have no other opportunity to be addressed.

Implementing a management review process in a company requires the following steps to be taken:

- Define who constitutes the top management of the company. Normally, this comprises the senior most executives who have the ultimate responsibility for decision making in the company.
- Define the periodicity of management review. Avoid too frequent reviews (one to two months) or too infrequent reviews (more than 12 months).
- Create a measuring and monitoring system that will enable the complete EMS performance to be measured.
- The management representative collects, collates and presents this data as an input to the management review process. A sample EMS management review input report

is shown in *Appendix H*. An EMS input report is just as good as the data or facts that it contains. Thus, an input report containing specific and accurate facts and results of EMS performance can greatly improve the effectiveness of the review process.

- It is good practice (though not a requirement) to share the EMS performance review report amongst the top management team before the actual review meeting. Top management reviews each element of the EMS performance and determines its suitability, adequacy and effectiveness. An important consideration for the review should be to look for opportunities for improvement and actions that may be needed to realise those improvements.

- The EMS review process must result in decisions and actions that could relate to changes that will correct any identified system deficiencies, or to bring further improvement to the EMS. A good management review should come up with clear decisions on what, when and who shall take the necessary actions to make corrections or improvements in the EMS system.

- Maintenance of the EMS management review records is a mandatory requirement. These records could consist of the presented input report (*see Appendix H*) and the outcomes of the review in terms of decisions and actions taken by the management.

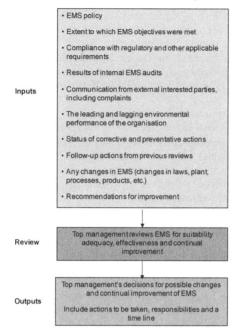

Figure 8: EMS management review process

Continual improvement

While 'continual improvement' of EMS is a mandatory requirement of the ISO14001 standard, it is not explicitly stated as to how it can be achieved. Looking closely, one can realise several EMS elements that suggest and also provide inputs to the continual improvement process. Let us follow the trail of all that has so far been done in establishing an EMS and see how different elements create opportunities for continual improvement of EMS.

- The EMS policy explicitly states top management's commitment towards continual improvement.

- Determining significant EMS aspects identifies those that require additional steps to be taken – and hence improvement of EMS.
- The demand for regulatory compliance requires an organisation to improve its environmental performance, so as to keep itself well within the specified regulatory limits.
- Environmental objectives, targets and programmes provide a formal process of continual improvement.
- Operational controls help eliminate, reduce or prevent the potential environmental impacts. Improving the effectiveness of operational controls or introducing additional controls is an ongoing aspect of the continual improvement process.
- Measurement and monitoring processes provide specific performance data to identify deficiencies and enable setting up of realistic improvement targets.
- Corrective and preventative actions to avoid recurrence of existing and occurrence of potential non-conformities lead to further improvement of EMS.
- The management review process takes a holistic view of EMS. It identifies deficiencies and considers possibilities for continual improvement.

Continual improvement is the final step in the Plan-Do-Check-Act (PDCA) cycle. It reflects the true spirit of the ISO14001 standard, which lies in not just establishing an EMS, but also in continually making it better and more effective.

CHAPTER 13: GREEN INITIATIVES

The term 'green initiative' may be referred to as 'the schemes, projects or programmes undertaken for the betterment of the environment', so as to eliminate or reduce the environmental footprint.

The entire eco-system is facing a multitude of challenges caused by industrialisation, urbanisation and other activities that are a stress on the environment. Environmental degradation caused by pollution of air, water, land and atmosphere is considered a key reason for changes in climate, food shortages, extinction of flora and fauna, as well as many types of diseases. Industrialisation and commercial activities have been the biggest contributors in environmental degradation. The impacts are loud enough to convey a very strong message – environmental management is no longer a matter of choice. It ought to be considered at each stage and for each business activity of an organisation.

Green initiatives, therefore, include efforts in eliminating, reversing or reducing the adverse environmental impacts of an organisation's products, processes, activities and services.

Figure 9 describes a model to develop an 'end-to-end' green business strategy:

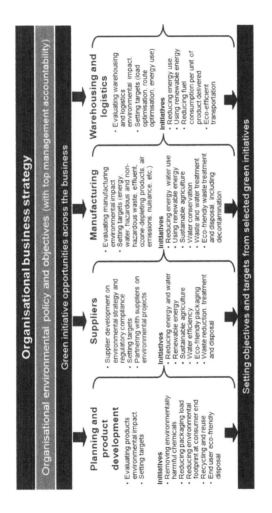

Organisational business strategy

Organisational environmental policy and objectives (with top management accountability)

Green initiative opportunities across the business

Planning and product development

· Evaluating products environmental impact
· Setting targets

Initiatives

· Removing environmentally harmful chemicals
· Reducing packaging load
· Reducing environmental footprint at consumer end
· Recycling and reuse
· End user eco-friendly disposal

Suppliers

· Supplier development on environmental strategy and regulatory compliance
· Setting targets
· Partnering with suppliers on environmental projects

Initiatives

· Reducing energy and water
· Renewable energy
· Sustainable agriculture
· Water efficiency
· Eco-friendly packaging
· Waste reduction, treatment and disposal

Manufacturing

· Evaluating manufacturing environmental impact
· Setting targets (energy, water, hazardous and non-hazardous waste, effluent, ozone-depleting products, air emissions, nuisance, etc.)

Initiatives

· Reducing energy, water use
· Using renewable energy
· Sustainable agriculture
· Water conservation
· Waste and water treatment
· Eco-friendly waste treatment and disposal, including decontamination

Warehousing and logistics

· Evaluating warehousing and logistics environmental impact
· Setting targets (load optimisation, route optimisation, energy use)

Initiatives

· Reducing energy use
· Using renewable energy
· Reducing fuel consumption per unit of product delivered
· Eco-efficient transportation

Setting objectives and targets from selected green initiatives

Figure 9: Green business strategy model

13: Green Initiatives

The following are a few examples of green initiatives that may be taken by different business sectors for reducing the environmental impacts of their operation.

IT industry:

- energy efficient computers, printers and other IT equipments with auto-sleep (low energy) mode when not in use
- developments of products run by solar energy
- recycling plastic, cartridges, toners, etc.

Packaging:

- purchasing paper and board material only from those suppliers who are purchasing their raw material from sustainable forests
- eco-friendly packaging with 100% recycling and bio-degradable options
- removing unnecessary packaging through improved design (e.g. air-shell packaging).

Offices and administration:

- using renewable energy (solar panels)
- eco-friendly designs to use sunlight in place of artificial lights
- using teleconferencing or videoconferencing to avoid road and air travel
- late sitting control to minimise air-conditioning or heating load
- off-hours energy optimisation (only security, IT network and fire-alarm system may need power backup, instead of a whole office)
- motion sensor lighting
- carpooling
- eliminating the use of disposable plastic bottles for drinking water
- encouraging the use of bicycles in place of company cars.

Warehousing and transportation:

- warehousing design to maximise use of daylight
- using renewable energy (solar/wind)
- reducing fuel consumed per unit of product delivered to customer by route or mode optimisation.

General:

- eliminating lead from petrol
- investment in renewable energy projects (solar, wind, geo-thermal, etc.)
- development of bio-fuels from agricultural waste or non-edible plantation (e.g. Jatropha)
- heat recovery projects (flare gases recovery and power generation projects, etc.)
- engaging communities on environmental issues (awareness programmes, eco-friendly disposal techniques, reuse and recycling, drip irrigation techniques, reforestation programmes, discontinuation of use of disposable plastic water bottles, etc.).

Consumer goods and foods:

- developing products with less environmental impacts (detergents that consume less water while washing clothes, recyclable and/or bio-degradable packaging)
- reducing the use of natural resources (water, fossil fuels, etc.)
- using 'pigging techniques' for waste and water reduction in changeovers
- eliminating marine pollutants from detergents, soaps and shampoos, etc. and replacing them with alternatives which are friendly to aquatic life
- replacing non-biodegradable plastic with bio-degradable or other recyclable alternatives
- eco-friendly waste disposal (site decontamination during acquisitions and closures, used packaging collection and recycling system, etc.).

Miscellaneous industries:

- lead free paints

- chrome recovery and recycling in leather industry
- ozone friendly refrigerants
- fuel efficient automobiles
- using bio-mass in boilers, furnaces and for other heating requirements
- using cleaner fuels with less significant emission impacts (e.g. replacing furnace oil boiler fuel with LPG or natural gas to reduce sulphur oxide emissions)
- using waste/bio-mass for power generation
- carbon trading.

Briefly, green initiatives should become the core of an organisation's environmental management system. They help reduce the carbon footprint, prevent pollution and create a more sustainable environment. They enable an organisation to go beyond the minimum requirement of regulatory compliance and make a larger contribution to the betterment of environment and society.

APPENDIX A: SAMPLE PROCEDURE FOR IDENTIFICATION OF ENVIRONMENTAL ASPECTS

Purpose

To define a process for identification of environmental aspects and impacts and determine those that have or can have significant environmental impacts. The procedure is applicable to all processes, products and activities carried by Eco-Friendly Inc. (EFI).

Responsibilities

Manager <   > is responsible for the following activities:

- identification of environmental aspects and those that have significant impacts
- maintenance and upkeep of significant aspect register.

Procedure

- Make an inventory of all processes, products and activities (routine, non-routine and emergency) performed by EFI.
- Identify inputs and outputs of each process, product and activity using a black box approach (as shown in *Figure 4*).
- Identify environmental aspects associated with inputs and outputs. Consider the following sources while identifying aspects/impacts:
    o observations, examination, brainstorming
    o process flow diagrams
    o material safety data sheets
    o data from previous incidents, accidents, spills, emissions
    o views of interested parties (records of external communication)
    o applicable legal and regulatory requirements
    o results of testing and analysis

- o input/output (mass balance)
- o utility bills
- o waste hauling records.
- Define the environmental impact of each aspect.
- Rank each impact on a scale. While determining the scale of an impact, give due consideration to controls already in place, severity, frequency, legal requirements, and impact on company image (*see Table 1*).

Significance criteria	Rating scheme
Legal liabilities: is the aspect regulated?	Low (1): not regulated High (4): regulated
Public / image concerns	Low (1) Medium (2) High (3) Very high: (4)
Difficulty or cost of changing the impact	Low (1) Medium (2) High (3) Very high (4)
Frequency: what is the frequency of occurrence of this environmental aspect?	Low (1): could be once in 10 years Medium (2): less than once a year High (3): every few months Very high (4): occurs monthly or more frequently

Significance criteria	Rating scheme
Severity: what is the overall severity (scale, harm to environments, duration)?	Low (1) Medium (2) High (3) Catastrophic (4)
Degree of controls already in place	Slight degree of control (4) Moderate degree of control (3) Medium degree of control (2) High degree of control (1)

Table 1: Ranking scale of impacts

- Use the format shown in *Table 2* for recording aspects and impacts.
- Calculate the average of all six impact-ratings. A score of two or above will be considered a significant environmental impact.
- Document aspects and impacts in a register of significant environmental aspects (*see Table 2*).
- Review and keep updated the register of significant environmental aspects as an ongoing activity (at least once every year). Also review whenever new aspects are identified, when an environmental incident takes place, when laws are changed, or whenever processes and activities are added or modified.

Records

The following records must be kept:

- a register of significant environmental aspects
- competence records for the environmental assessment team.

Activity product service				
Aspect				
Impact				
(a)	Degree of controls already in place			
(b)	Legal liability			
(c)	Public, image concerns			
(d)	Cost / difficulty of changing the impact			
(e)	Severity			
(f)	Frequency			
Overall score = Average (a:f) Significant if score > 2				

Table 2: Register of significant environmental aspects

APPENDIX B: SAMPLE PROCEDURE FOR INTERNAL AND EXTERNAL COMMUNICATION

Purpose

To define a process for internal and external communication on environmental aspects and the EMS of Eco-Friendly Inc. (EFI).

Responsibilities

Manager <   > is responsible for internal EMS communication.

Manager <   > is responsible for external EMS communication.

Procedure

Manager <   > ensures that a two-way communication process relating to environmental issues is established between personnel at all levels in the organisation. This includes visitors and contractors working on site. These processes shall ensure that the following EMS related facts, reports, instructions and awareness procedures (as applicable) are communicated to all personnel:

- environmental issues
- significant environmental aspects
- eco-friendly initiatives and environmental objectives
- reporting of environmental incidents using e-mail and drop box
- pollution prevention, waste management, recycling and reuse
- emergency procedures
- applicable operational controls, procedures and instructions
- EMS reports and results of EMS performance communicated to concerned managers and top management

- applicable legal and other requirements subscribed to by the organisation which need to be known by those responsible for measuring, monitoring or ensuring compliance.

There shall be at least two awareness sessions per year on each of the above topics, while the regulatory requirements and changes in procedures will be communicated immediately after receipt of a change.

Manager < > ensures that a two-way communication process relating to external communication is established. The external communication process shall ensure receipt, response and recording of all communication relating to environmental issues. This may involve:

- communication with NGOs, environmental groups and communities
- communication with government, regulatory and environmental protection agencies
- communication relating to permits, licences and fines
- communication with press and other media
- reporting of mandatory environmental data to environmental agencies and corporate bodies.

Records

Records that must be kept include records of receipts and responses to all external communications.

APPENDIX C: SAMPLE PROCEDURE FOR CONTROL OF DOCUMENTS AND RECORDS

Document no. EFI-01

Revision: 0

Revision date: dd/mm/yy

Purpose

This procedure defines the mechanism for development, approval, review, updating, distribution and maintenance of controlled documents used in EFI's environment management system (EMS). It also includes mechanisms for identification, preservation, maintenance, retention and disposal of records.

Responsibility

Manager <   > has the overall responsibility to ensure implementation of this procedure.

Procedure

Management of controlled documents

- All EMS documents shall bear a unique identification number. This shall be EFI-01, 02, 03 … .
- Manager <   > shall allocate a unique number to each document.
- Manager <   > ensures that a master list (EFI-02) of all EMS controlled documents is maintained, which identifies each document and its current revision status. The same will be done for documents of external origin.
- Manager <   > ensures that the documents are distributed so as to be available and accessible to all those who need to use them.
- EMS documents at EFI shall be approved by the following personnel.

Document title	Approving authority
EMS manual	Company head < >
EMS policy	Company head < >
EMS objective and targets	Company head < >
EMS programmes	Manager < >
EMS procedures	Manager < >
Standard operating procedures (or work instructions)	Manager < >
EMS forms for recording results and/or data	Manager < >

Table 3: Document approval responsibilities

- Documents are assigned a revision number and date to indicate their latest revision status.
- Those issued with controlled documents must ensure that they remain available and legible.
- Manager < > ensures that obsolete documents are promptly removed from all points of issue. Obsolete documents will be segregated to prevent unintended use. Manager < > shall decide if an obsolete document is to be destroyed or retained for historical purposes. If retained, the document shall be stamped as 'obsolete document' in order to prevent its unintended use.

- Changes in documentation may be initiated by anyone who identifies or proposes the need for a change.
- Changes to documents must be reviewed and approved by the same authority that had reviewed and approved the original document.
- Changes in documents shall be made easily noticeable by writing the changed text in ***bold and italic*** font.

Management of records

- The retention period of each record and the responsibility for record maintenance is defined at EFI-03. The legal and company requirements are considered while establishing retention periods of records.
- Each record holder is responsible for ensuring that the records are readily available and legible. They are kept safe and prevented from loss or damage.
- Records must be traceable by including information such as events, dates, persons and approvals.
- Records that have completed their retention period are disposed off. Record holders may revise retention periods, where necessary, and changes made to EFI-03 accordingly.
- The following controls are applicable for electronically maintained records:
  - Manager <   > shall ensure that access and authorisation is controlled through passwords and/or access codes.
  - Data loss is prevented by ensuring regular back-ups and data corruption is prevented by an online anti-virus scanning programme.
  - Manager < > shall ensure that data is backed up and maintained at a remote location on data storage devices.

Records

Record no.	Record name	Maintained by	Retention period
EFI-02	List of documents	Manager < >	2 years
EFI-03	List of records	Manager < >	2 years

Approved by: ....

Table 4: Example record maintenance

APPENDIX D: DOCUMENTS REQUIRED BY ISO14001

Clause	Documents required by the standard
4.2	Environmental policy
4.3.1	Procedure(s) for environmental aspects and impacts assessment
4.3.2	Procedure(s) for legal and other requirements
4.3.3	Environmental objectives, targets and programmes
4.4.1	Documented roles, responsibilities and authorities for EMS
4.4.2	Procedure(s) for internal and external communication
4.4.3	Procedure(s) for competence, awareness and training

4.4.4	A document that describes the scope and description of the main elements of EMS and their interactions
4.4.5	Procedure(s) for document control
4.4.6	• Documented procedures to control situations pertaining to significant environmental aspects • Documented procedures for purchase of goods and services pertaining to significant environmental aspects and communication thereof to suppliers and contractors
4.4.7	Procedure(s) for emergency preparedness and response
4.5.1	Procedure(s) for monitoring and measurement
4.5.2.1 and 4.5.2.2	Procedure(s) for periodic evaluation compliance with applicable legal and other requirements

4.5.3	Procedure(s) for non-conformity, corrective and preventative actions
4.5.4	Procedure(s) for control of records
4.5.5 b	Procedure(s) for internal EMS audit

APPENDIX E: RECORDS REQUIRED BY ISO14001

Clause	Topic	Records required by the standard
4.3.1	Environmental aspects	Results of environmental aspects and impacts assessment
4.4.2	Competence, training and awareness	• Competence needs/criteria of personnel performing tasks having significant environmental aspects • Training records
4.4.3	Communication	Decisions on communications with external interested parties
4.5.1	Monitoring and measurement	• Information to monitor performance, operational controls, • conformance to objectives and targets • Equipment

		calibration records
4.5.2.1	Evaluation of compliance	Results of periodic evaluation compliance with applicable regulatory requirements
4.5.2.2	Evaluation of compliance	Results of periodic evaluation of compliance with other applicable environmental requirements
4.5.3	Non-conformity, corrective and preventative actions	Corrective and preventative actions taken
4.5.5 b	Internal audit	Results of EMS audit
4.6	Management review	Records of the management review

APPENDIX F: SAMPLE FORMAT FOR A NON-CONFORMITY REPORT (NCR)

NCR no:	NCR date:
Reference no. of document against which this non-conformity is raised: company procedure / ISO14001 / legal requirement / complaint from interested party / other:	
Describe non-conformity: Signed: Date:	

Action taken to correct the non-conformity (include actions taken to mitigate environmental aspects, if any):

Signed:

Date:

Root cause(s)

Actions taken to eliminate root cause(s) to avoid recurrence:

Signed:

Date:

Review of corrective actions for
effectiveness:

Signed:

Date:

APPENDIX G: SAMPLE PROCEDURE FOR INTERNAL EMS AUDIT

Purpose

To define the process and responsibilities for planning, conducting, reporting and follow-up of internal EMS audits at Eco-Friendly Inc. (EFI)

Responsibilities

Manager <   > has the overall responsibility to:

- plan internal EMS audits
- ensure auditor competency and independence
- designate auditors for specific audits
- ensure regulatory compliance is also audited
- monitor the conduct of audits
- follow up and report the results of audits to senior management.

Procedure

Planning

- All departments of EFI shall be audited against all elements of the standard at least once every year. Additional audits may be scheduled considering the environmental significance of activities and the results of previous audits.
- Manager < > shall prepare an audit plan for each audit and communicate it to the auditors and auditees at least three weeks prior to audit.

- The audit plan defines:
  - audit scope and criteria
  - audit team members and the functions to be audited
  - audit dates, times, and any other requirements
  - responsibilities for writing the audit report and taking follow-up actions.

Responsibilities / qualifications

Manager <   > shall nominate a lead auditor and at least one auditor as the audit team for each audit. The auditors would be considered suitable to conduct an internal EMS audit if they meet the following conditions:

- they meet auditor competence requirements defined in the training procedure of EFI
- they are independent of the activity and/or department being audited
- they have participated in at least two audits as an observer auditor.

Internal EMS audit process

- EMS audits will be conducted primarily through interviews, observing physical conditions and checking documents and records.
- The audit team will conduct short opening and closing meetings with the departmental head of the area that is being audited, to explain the scope and methodology of the audit.
- Auditors will document non-conformities and hand them over to the management of the area under audit. A copy of the non-conformity report is given to Manager <   > for record and follow-up.
- Responsibility for determining root cause(s) and taking corrective actions will reside with the functional area managers where findings occurred. Management representatives should be requested to co-ordinate where required.

- The lead auditor (unless otherwise specified by Manager < >) should follow up to ensure that the corrective actions are completed by the agreed-upon dates. The EMS audit is closed when it is established that the corrective actions are effective and have been fully implemented.

Audit report

When the audit is complete, the lead auditor will complete the audit report and make it available to the Manager < > and the functional area manager for the area(s) audited.

Audit as input to the management review

Manager < > shall present the results of the audit and the status of the corrective actions to the top management of EFI as an input to the management review process. Any non-conformities that have not been fully implemented will continue to be monitored, and a status report will be provided until the corrective action is fully implemented.

Records

Records that must be kept include:

- an audit plan
- audit non-conformity reports
- audit report.

APPENDIX H: SAMPLE INPUT REPORT FOR EMS MANAGEMENT REVIEW

Input report for the management review to be conducted on 12-07-2010 by the top management of Eco-Friendly Inc. (EFI).

Extent to which EMS objectives and targets were met

EFI had established two EMS objectives at the beginning of 2010. These were:

- **The water consumption in the factory shall be reduced from 15,000 gallons per month to 12,000 gallons per month by December 2010**
  Status: this objective has been fully achieved and our current monthly water consumption has been reduced to 11,000 gallons per month.
- **Reduction of carbon emissions by 2% by December 2011**
  Status: six targets were identified for achievement of this objective: three for 2010 and three for 2011. The three targets for 2010 (carbon emission study, procurement of carbon reduction equipment and optimising the combustion process of the two boilers) have been achieved.

Compliance with regulatory and other applicable requirements

EFI is in compliance with all applicable regulatory requirements relating to emissions, effluents, solid waste and permit renewals. This was reconfirmed in the six-monthly compliance audit conducted in June 2010. Test results showing EFI performance (emissions, effluents, hazardous waste and permits) against applicable regulatory requirements are attached with this report.

Results of internal EMS audits

Two EMS audits were carried in 2010. A complete system audit in February 2010 and an EMS audit of the production department in May 2010.

Complete system audit – February 2010

It was a four man-day audit carried out by trained internal auditors. The audit confirmed that EFI was in complete compliance with all regulatory requirements. The system was well implemented and the objectives and targets were being met. The audit also identified one non-conformity. Details are given below:

- **Non-conformity:** scrubber used for reducing emission of sulphur oxide in Chimney No. 2 was inoperative for past five weeks.
- **Root cause:** ineffective maintenance programme and lack of awareness amongst scrubber maintenance personnel.
- **Corrective actions taken:**
  o scrubber repaired and re-installed
  o all other scrubbers checked for effective working
  o the maintenance system was reviewed and it was ensured that all pollution prevention equipment would be identified and a maintenance plan made to ensure ongoing preventative maintenance (*Procedure EFI-07, Rev. 2* was revised to include the new requirements)
  o training need identification was revisited and the training requirements for pollution prevention equipment were identified for all maintenance personnel (the new training requirements were included in the 2010-2011 training calendar).

Production department audit – May 2010

It was a two man-day audit carried out by trained internal auditors for the production department only. The audit confirmed that EMS operational controls were well in place.

The audit also identified one non-conformity. Details are provided below:

- **Non-conformity:** no operational controls deployed for potential spillage or leak from oil drums kept in store.
- **Root cause:**
  - o inadequate assessment of significant impacts in case of emergency situations
  - o inadequate measuring and monitoring
  - o lack of awareness of operational controls.

- **Corrective actions taken:**
  - o tiled surface prepared for areas where drums are kept to cater for drainage of potential spillage and leakage
  - o inspection for incoming drums introduced to separate any damaged or leaking drums
  - o purchase process modified (*EFI-05, Rev. 4*).
  - o training need identification was revisited and the training requirements for EMS operational controls were identified for all concerned persons (new training requirements were included in the 2010-2011 training calendar)
  - o other lube oil storage locations were inspected to ensure that similar controls are also implemented in those locations
  - o spill kits placed in each lube oil storage location to be used for containment in case of spills (personnel also trained in the use of spill kits).

Communication from external interested parties, including complaints

Since the last management review meeting there was one complaint and one query received from interested parties. The communication received and actions taken were as follows:

- **Communication:** complaint received from local road-traffic control department, received 10 June 2010. The complaint related to spillage and leaks from EFI's vehicles while travelling between EFI and the customers' premises.

Action: EFI raised a non-conformity report. Lack of vehicle maintenance and inadequate inspection of vehicles prior to departure from factory were identified as the root causes. Corrective actions were taken to introduce regular vehicle inspections as well as pre-departure vehicle checks. A response was sent to the traffic control department explaining all the corrective actions taken by EFI.

- **Communication:** 12 April 2010, 'The Green Initiatives', an NGO working towards environmental protection, sent a query asking if the effluent discharged by EFI met the biological oxygen demand (BOD) limits of 30 mg/litre.

  Action: as it is the policy of EFI to disclose its environmental performance (if specifically asked for by an interested party), a response was sent stating that the BOD value of EFI effluent is 25 mg/litre, which is well within the stated limits.

Environmental performance

The environmental performance as judged from lagging environmental performance indicators.

Lagging parameters (based on 50,000 tons of production from July 2009 to June 2010)	Performance
Amount of hazardous waste generated	2000 kg
Quantity of toxic chemicals released	Nil
Number of notices of violation	Nil
Amount of fuel used	5000 gallons

Amount of water used	11,000 gallons per month
Ozone depleting substances in use (relate to old versions of air conditioning units)	6
Hazardous air pollutants (HAPs) released to air	20 pounds
Spills of oil or hazardous substances (notified to regulatory bodies and corrective actions taken)	1
Energy usage/unit of product	0.23 kilo watt hour

Table 5: Lagging EMS performance indicators

Leading parameter	Performance
Number of purchase reviews completed for environmental aspects	3
Number of voluntary initiatives participated in	2
Number of community outreach activities	2 half-day sessions
Number of internal self assessments completed	2
Number of environmental management reviews completed	2
Regulatory issues identified proactively and resolved	1
Number of EMS training courses completed	9

Table 6: Leading EMS performance parameters

Status of corrective and preventative actions

- Corrective actions initiated … 3
  Current status … all closed out. Results verified for effectiveness.
- Preventative actions initiated … 1
  Current status … action pending due to delay in budget approval.

Follow-up actions from previous reviews

Previous review decisions included two items:

- Revision of contractor management procedure to include extending EMS controls to those contractors working for EFI outside company premises. Completed through *EFI-09, Rev. 3.*
- Building a wall to contain generator noise from disturbing the neighbourhood residents. This has been accomplished and the neighbour community is fully satisfied with the new arrangement.

Any changes in EMS or circumstances that could relate to environmental aspects

Two changes have been introduced that have a potential for new or changed environmental aspects in the company. These are:

- construction of a new warehouse for storage of paints and epoxies
- introduction of 50 new printers that could be generating hazardous solid waste (toners and cartridges) in the weeks to come.

EMS policy

The EMS policy of EFI was last revised in June 2009. The policy is enclosed for review and possible changes by top management.

Recommendations for improvement

Three recommendations are being made for consideration by top management for continual improvement of EMS. These are:

- making a new EMS objective for reducing the carbon footprint of the company
- providing training on the corrective and preventative action process to all managers
- purchase of BOD/COD testing equipment so that testing of outgoing effluent can be carried out more frequently to exercise ongoing control over these parameters.

Signed:

Management representative (EMS)

BIBLIOGRAPHIC NOTES

ISO14001:2004 *Environmental management systems – Requirements with guidance for use*: *http://www.iso.org/iso/catalogue_detail?csnumber=31807*.

ISO19011:2002 *Guidelines for quality and/or environmental management systems auditing*: *http://www.iso.org/iso/catalogue_detail.htm?csnumber=31169*.

ITG RESOURCES

IT Governance Ltd. sources, creates and delivers products and services to meet the real-world, evolving IT governance needs of today's organisations, directors, managers and practitioners.

The ITG website (*www.itgovernance.co.uk*) is the international one-stop-shop for corporate and IT governance information, advice, guidance, books, tools, training and consultancy.

www.itgovernance.co.uk/catalog/346 is the information page on our website for our ISO14000 resources.

Other Websites

Books and tools published by IT Governance Publishing (ITGP) are available from all business booksellers and are also immediately available from the following websites:

www.itgovernance.co.uk/catalog/355 provides information and online purchasing facilities for every currently available book published by ITGP.

www.itgovernanceusa.com is a US$-based website that delivers the full range of IT Governance products to North America, and ships from within the continental US.

www.itgovernanceasia.com provides a selected range of ITGP products specifically for customers in South Asia.

www.27001.com is the IT Governance Ltd. website that deals specifically with information security management, and ships from within the continental US.

Pocket Guides

For full details of the entire range of pocket guides, simply follow the links at:
www.itgovernance.co.uk/publishing.aspx.

Toolkits

ITG's unique range of toolkits includes the IT Governance Framework Toolkit, which contains all the tools and guidance that you will need in order to develop and implement an appropriate IT governance framework for your organisation. Full details can be found at *www.itgovernance.co.uk/ products/519*.

For a free paper on how to use the proprietary Calder-Moir IT Governance Framework, and for a free trial version of the toolkit, see:
www.itgovernance.co.uk/calder_moir.aspx.

There is also a wide range of toolkits to simplify implementation of management systems, such as an ISO/IEC 27001 ISMS or a BS25999 BCMS, and these can all be viewed and purchased online at: *http://www.itgovernance.co.uk/catalog/1.*

Best Practice Reports

ITG's range of Best Practice Reports is now at: *www.itgovernance.co.uk/best-practice-reports.aspx*. These offer you essential, pertinent, expertly researched information on an increasing number of key issues including Web 2.0 and Green IT.

Training and Consultancy

IT Governance also offers training and consultancy services across the entire spectrum of disciplines in the information governance arena. Details of training courses can be accessed at *www.itgovernance.co.uk/training.aspx* and descriptions of our consultancy services can be found at *http://www.itgovernance.co.uk/consulting.aspx*.
Why not contact us to see how we could help you and your organisation?

Newsletter

IT governance is one of the hottest topics in business today, not least because it is also the fastest moving, so what better way to keep up than by subscribing to ITG's free monthly newsletter *Sentinel*? It provides monthly updates and resources across the whole spectrum of IT governance subject matter, including risk management, information security, ITIL and IT service management, project governance, compliance and so much more. Subscribe for your free copy at: *www.itgovernance.co.uk/newsletter.aspx*.

Lightning Source UK Ltd.
Milton Keynes UK
UKOW07f1829230115

245035UK00015B/317/P